I0504224

THE ART OF SELLING

HOW TO BECOME A TOPNOTCH SALESPERSON

ANTHONY EKANEM

ISBN 978-1-68538-778-5

Contents

Preface

On average, a person encounters about three salespersons in a day. Your phone will ring one sunny morning; a jovial salesperson is on the other end of the line selling you cruise vacation tickets. As you condition yourself for a relaxing nap, somebody begins knocking on your door, and when you open it, an insurance salesman is right at your face smiling his heart out. You try to sort out your emails before going to bed, and you noticed that half of them are promotional newsletters.

You might be tired of salespeople yourself. You might have hated the mere sight of one. But do you know that it is one of the most rewarding jobs around? Well, not unless you can become the next President of the United States, but then, I could be wrong.

Salespeople are the very individuals who move the company. Their job is to market the products and make the company flourish in the process. If a salesperson is not able to do his job well, then the rest of the company will fall. The CEO, down to the rank-and-file employees, will soon be out of their jobs.

Do you see now how powerful salespeople can be? And because of this alone, they are quite indispensable in any organisation. For a salesperson, every sale merits a commission. And for their every good performance, income spiffs and special bonuses, who then would not want to be a salesperson and become wealthy and successful?

Do you now want to be involved in sales? If you still don't feel up for it, take this. It is in selling where the money lies. You do not even have to invest too much, nor would you need any capital upfront. All you needed is the right skills and the correct attitude for the job. That is precisely what this book is going to give you. After you've gone through this book as a whole, you will become a top-notch salesperson - a salesperson who can sell anything and everything under the sun, from a shiny new car to a multi-coloured checkered coat and tie collection.

Whatever product you are selling won't matter at all. Your merchandise, service, or goods will all be sold in a matter of minutes, hours, or days, depending upon their complexity and worth. And you will achieve your first million sooner than you have ever expected.

Almost no one is born to become a top-notch salesperson, although some may have "natural" talents in selling. They are all trained to become one. And there are no stringent pre-requisites for that. All you need is the willingness and the desire to succeed. Once you have that, you will get a good focus on your goal. You will notice that everything simply falls into place. You will become a master when it comes to selling.

Expect that selling is something that you can do well. Everybody can become successful in the field of sales. People go to the market each day. They shop for the food that they will eat and the things they will use. You see, almost every place is a marketplace. Selling is simply a part of our lives. Most of the time, you are on the buying end. But this time around, you are on the selling end. The bottom line is that we are usually involved in a selling deal. And because of that, you must have seen good salespeople at work, right? Try to observe how they can make people buy their pieces of stuff or even ideas. They have a particular ability that makes them good at their job.

As you read this book, that outstanding salesperson can be you. The things written here will help you, if not transform you into becoming an excellent salesperson in just a brief period. This book is for everyone, no matter whether it is your first time selling or you have any experience in selling before. And for those who had tried their hands at selling and didn't do well, it doesn't matter what your sales record is before. You could have been your company's most terrible salesperson. But as Gene Fowler, a famous writer, and actor, had said, "I am the world's worst salesperson; therefore, I must make it easy for people to buy."

As we start your preparation to become a top-notch salesperson, try to maintain a small note pad where you can list the answer to the questions, exercises, and the rest of the pointers contained in this book. Doing so will expedite the entire learning process and make you the top-notch seller that you really are.

CHAPTER ONE

Understanding the Selling Market

Before gearing up to sell, you must understand one essential thing in selling – and that's your potential market. The potential market is simply defined as a group of people who could be interested in the product or services that you are offering. These are the people to whom you will be selling your products, and apparently, their roles are critical.

Whatever product you are advertising, there is only one thing to keep in mind: you have to know who your target market is. It is not a good suggestion to sell beauty creams and makeup in a car-racing magazine, would it? Well, not unless you want to utilise whatever media you can put your hands on. But still, doing that is an incredible idea.

Who Are Your Target Market?

For you to know exactly where to sell, you have to analyse your product first. And for you to do that, answer these ten simple questions:

1. Who are the direct beneficiaries of the product or service you are selling?

2. Are there any indirect beneficiaries? If so, who are they?

3. Who can afford these products? What's the income bracket of the persons who are willing to buy them?

4. Would these people prefer to buy them in cash or through other payment methods, like a credit card or check? Do they have to sign a loan or an instalment plan agreement before purchasing?

5. Where and how exactly are these products used? At home? In schools? At work?

6. Who are the people that are most likely to buy? Male or female? Married or single? Young or old?

7. Is the product a necessity, or is it just a luxury?

8. Is the demand for the product seasonal, or will it be the same all year round?

9. Are potential customers already aware of this product, or is it something new and innovative?

10. Do these people have to gather decision-making data, or would they be capable of buying at the spur of the moment?

These ten straightforward questions would effectively take you right in front of the people where a big chunk of revenues will be coming from. After listing all the definite answers to the questions, you should have a clear idea of where your potential markets are. You should then be able to have a good idea as to what method of attack you should use for your every target market.

Segregating Your Market

Still referring to the answers you have for the questions above, you may notice that you have a rather diverse group of buyers. Your product may cater for a big group of people, young and old, male or female. Segregating your market is essential so that you will be able to cater to their individual needs. According to several pieces of research, doing that will take you closer to your prospective buyers and, eventually, to sales and profit.

To successfully segregate your market, here are the things that you have to remember:

1. **Determine the distinctive needs of each group of people.**

For sure, male executives buying your product will have at least one different reason from single mothers who will be buying it. Although you are selling the same goods to these two sets of different people, the presence of their individual needs and benefits remains. This is something that you have to capitalise on as you plan your sales pitch.

2. **Conduct a research.**

You won't effectively know your target market if you are just guessing what their needs and wants might be. You have to know them for sure and should not settle for the but's, if's, and maybe's. Send out a survey. Consult with the experts and read a lot about these people and be adequately informed. Know how your competitors do it. Alternatively, if your budget allows it, hire a company to do all of these for you. Then test your market. The main idea here is for you to be reasonably assured that you are following the right strategy.

3. **Say only the "proper" things.**

You have to speak the particular group's language. If you intend to sell to the young or the teenagers, you have to talk like one of them and not like strict parents asking them to do this and do that. Speak as if you are a teenager yourself. Know what their heart's desires are. And give those to them exactly. You should talk like a member of their group, and not an outsider wanting to be a part of it. Your target market will most likely detect a hoax when they smell one. And the effects of that are rather unappealing.

Focusing on Your Market

Now that you know all your potential markets, you have to cater to each of their peculiar needs. This is commonly referred to as niche marketing. A niche market is simply a specific portion of a bigger market. It is nothing but a narrowed group of probable customers that is often overlooked by a mainstream provider.

To make things clearer, let us use a concrete example. If your business is all about home insurance, divide that into several niches like mansion house insurance, bungalow insurance, and condominium unit insurance. That way, you will be able to focus more on your segregated market. By following the niche concept, you are sure to bundle the mansion house insurance package with all the necessary provisions and even freebies that a mansion owner will be glad to own, and which he might not get from any other general insurance companies. Going into niches would enable you to put up the quality of your products. And more people will certainly go to you too, thinking that you are the expert they need.

Always remember that every niche market has its own needs and requirements. That is going to be your focus. For you to successfully meet all their specific needs, the first thing that you have to do is to select a profitable niche carefully. Choosing the right niche starts with it all. When choosing, consider its profitability. Keep in mind that a niche group of potential customers is relatively small, so focus on a highly lucrative group of people.

Analyse your market to know who your competitors are. Are they offering niches as well? If they are not, then you are lucky. All you have to do is to choose one specific area and focus on that. If, unfortunately, they are offering niches as well, try to determine the area that is not yet serviced. Be creative. If your business is about home decors, a profitable niche is an exotic collection of decorative items from different countries all over the world, like Egypt or the Bahamas, for example. Your main goal is to be the best provider for that particular group. Maintain an inventory of the best products given at the best price.

So you will be guided appropriately when serving your respective niche, talk to real persons with real needs belonging to your chosen category. Look for an ideal customer. Ask him pertinent information as to what he expects to get about your line of products. Include in your query the things that he thinks he should not be getting as well as his suggestions as to how to make the whole thing better.

Going back to the home décor example, your ideal customer will be a well-travelled middle to upper-class homeowner. This person will have an idea as to what things you will be asking about and the things that you should know. He must have seen, and maybe even touched, exotic culture. He will be a reliable source of market information.

Then couple what you have found out from him with real market research. This has to be done to verify the information you have gathered. Is your ideal customer's taste the same as the rest of the community? Are his ideas feasible? Along with answering these questions, you should also be able to determine the right strategy for penetrating the market. Include the production costs as well as your close competitor's product line. You can do the market research yourself.

First, try to talk to more potential customers. Still using the home décor example, you can also read current home décor magazines to get market leads as to where your possible suppliers and buyers are. Search the Internet for sites that are more or less similar to your idea. By doing so, you will be able to adjust your market and products accordingly.

Finally, go deeper into the personal preferences of your potential customers. Know what qualities they look for and feel more about your line of product. For home decors, a good feature will be the history embodied in a particular item. Sell pieces that are reflective of a nation's tradition and culture. More people will surely come to you. When that happens, you need not go to your market anymore, and everything becomes simpler.

Other related product characteristics will be quality, price, convenience, or reliability. Once you have pinpointed that particular trait, which they regard highly the most, you are then assured of selling your products effortlessly. Selling has just become one step easier.

Using Analysis to Understand Your Market

Your success as a salesperson depends on your market's current saturation. Your customers will be divided amongst your competitors and other similar factors. For you to fully identify your market, try to answer these ten questions. They will guide you in your selling goals.

1. How many competitors exist in your market?

2. Which of them are new and which are already there for the longest time?

3. How many of them are bigger than your business?

4. How much do they affect your sales? Are you losing big profits because of them?

5. How do they price their products?

6. Are their products and services similar to or different from yours? In what way?

7. What advertising tools do they use? To what extent are those used?

8. Are they selling to the same customer group as yours? Do you have customer groups that they can't sell to yet?

9. How do your customers buy? What motivates them?

10. Do your competitors employ a significant number of salespeople? Do they use different selling techniques like door-to-door, retail outlets, telemarketing, direct mail, or business-to-business?

Once these questions are answered, you will not only be successful in analysing your customers. You will know more about your competitors, as well. And with all this knowledge, you will be able to plan and select the best selling method possible. By doing so, you will soon become a very successful salesperson.

The Ten Buying Drives

Customers buy for a reason. No matter how complex some of the reasons they throw at you may seem to be, most of the root of the ten primary buying motives are listed below. Capitalise on one or a combination of these motives, and you will successfully sell to your customers.

1. **Self-preservation**

Self-preservation corresponds to people's basic needs. These are the necessities such as food, clothing, shelter, and all products that relate to their health and safety. Business-wise, it means products that will help them in their jobs, making their work faster and easier to become more successful and highly effective employees. The question to answer then, is how does your product help your customers, either on a personal or business level? How does it fill their basic needs?

2. **Value**

With today's challenging economy, getting value for one's money is everybody's concern. People don't feel like buying something that is not worth their money. Most people are willing to pay any price for a good product. You then have to make sure you sell with integrity. That means you won't give your customers empty promises and false claims about your product. So, how will your product honestly accommodate your possible customer's needs and expectations?

3. Sex

Sex means you are appealing to the customer's femininity or masculinity. This corresponds to your product's ability to enhance its attractiveness and appeal to the opposite sex. People are naturally vain. They are willing to buy something that would make them a lot more attractive, more lovable, and more likeable than they currently are. What then, is your product's role in making your customers look better in front of other people?

4. Dreams

All people have dreams, aspirations, or even fantasies. And they all want to realise it or even to achieve something that even mildly resembles it. Early on in their lives, they have visions of what they should become, what they should own, and what their lifestyle should be. Dreams come in all shapes and forms. It means dreams can be big and high, but they could also be small and simple. Whatever dreams your customer might have, what does your product propose to fulfil them?

5. Emulation

Quite naturally, customers would like to be somebody they admire. Be it movie stars, celebrities, and members of the higher society, one thing holds. They would like to be associated, compared, or even be reminded of them.

They would like to have their idols' looks, their wealth, and their elegance. Some people think that by buying the products their favourite celebrity endorses, most of their qualities are going to rub off on them. So, is a well-known or reputable person endorsing your product? Better yet, how do you associate your product with somebody prominent?

6. Revenge Motives

Some customers would like to show the world that they are worth something good. This type of buying motive has both a good and a bad side. It is because while you want to bring out the best in them, you do it by evoking their innermost emotions of bitterness, insecurity, plainness, and mediocrity. This type of motivation is usually left unsaid because of the negative implications associated with it. Nevertheless, it is a compelling motive to buy. How sensitive are you to this motive, and how can your product help your customer in their goal to make even?

7. Style

As times go by, trends change. And to keep up in style is something customers would like to achieve. Customers do not want to be left out from the crowd and be considered yesterday's news. What they want is to fit in and be one with the people who are considered chic, trendy, and fashionable. Is your product the "in" thing today? Will owning it means you conform to today's changing world?

8. Knowledge

Information is power. This is the reason why self-help books and materials are making raves in the market. Owning them makes a person more prosperous, more skilled, and better informed. Some people are willing to go to greater heights just to know more about their hobbies, the things that fascinate them, or even the everyday things that work around them. Many people are still hungry for learning. If your product satisfies their hunger, you might as well appeal to this buying motive. Is your product going to be helpful in a way to your customer through information dissemination?

9. Elitism

Who would want to feel high and mighty? People would like to be regarded as elite or essential. If a particular product can give a sense of elitism to them, they will buy it. Examples of such products are jewellery, expensive apparel, a fast car, or a big house. Will owning your product give your customers the satisfaction of being one of the best?

10. Being Liked

The feeling of being admired or at least being accepted is enough to make a person tingle. Nobody would like to be embarrassed by not owning something everybody assumes to be "the thing". They don't want to be caught dead without something most of their friends own. There are also times they would like to start a trend themselves. And they can do it by getting a good product that would make them the subject of admiration or even envy. So, how will your product make somebody acceptable? How can it solicit the respect of others?

CHAPTER TWO

Setting Up and Realising Your Goal

Now, here is where all the hard work lies ahead. Well, let's omit the word "hard" there. Selling can be easy anyway, especially if you know what you are doing. To realise your goal as a salesperson, the first thing you have to do is to set it. What exactly do you want to achieve as one? Do you want to earn big cash? Millions? Or do you want to be a sales supervisor, then a sales director? Maybe being the company's vice president for sales is such a good idea after all, don't you think?

When it comes to setting goals, there is only one rule to remember - set a goal that is possible to achieve. There's nothing wrong with focusing on an extravagant goal, like being a sales division head. But it won't happen overnight, especially if you just started your job yesterday. It is better to set small, short-term goals and go from there. Achieve all these small goals one at a time, one after another, and you will undoubtedly wake up one morning on top of your career and with loads of money in your bank account at that.

Short-term goals are much easier to achieve. It takes lesser time and sometimes even lesser effort to accomplish a short-term goal. Short-term goals are mostly done in a matter of months or even days. Let's apply this concept and take college as an example. For you to finish college, you schedule yourself to attend university fairs and seminars. Doing that is a short-term goal, a small goal. Finishing college, on the other hand, is the long-term goal or the bigger goal.

Most people incorrectly set big dreams with their big goals. That's perfectly fine – no problem with that. But several people who are doing this get tired of pursuing their dream, and eventually, they give up. They became too weary of failing because they do not understand nor realise all the complexities associated with achieving those colossal goals.

It is always preferable, to begin with, small goals before you head on to take more significant challenges and dreams. Try splitting your big, long-term goals into several small but achievable short-term goals. When you look at your goals from that perspective, you will realise that your bigger goals become more attainable.

Let's use a concrete example again. Say you like to become a millionaire through selling. Make that your ultimate goal. Under that, make several short-term goals significant to your current position. Give yourself a month doing your selling with the simple goal of being able to pay the bills. If you have successfully achieved that, proceed to earn enough to pay the bills plus a number of your luxuries, like a monthly out-of-town vacation or a shopping spree perhaps. After those, and if you are still doing well in your craft, continue with the next set of goals. Aim to buy a house or a new car. Then make enough money to spend most of the holidays abroad with your family. Proceed to save a bundle for your retirement. Slowly, but indeed, you will eventually find your bank account with savings of seven figures, at least.

Now do your goal-setting activity. List one ultimate goal and make at least ten baby steps under it. And under each small goal, make several concrete steps to do on how you can achieve each goal. Then push yourself on achieving one goal after another. Don't skip any of your goals, and you will surely be on the right track.

Honing Your Face-to-Face Selling Skills

One way to realise your goal is to make sure that you sharpen your face-to-face selling skills. This is helpful if you have to do door-to-door selling, service sales, or customer service. To be an effective face-to-face seller, here are useful tips you have to follow:

1. **Make sure you have all the sales material at hand.**

Don't expect to make big sales if you are not prepared for everything. You always have to have the order forms, purchase orders, sales slips, selling materials, and specification sheets handy. Bring them wherever you go. Make sure you have extra copies of each in your car, your briefcase, desk, and counter. If you are always ready, you won't give your customer any room for second thoughts.

2. **Always stay well organised to make selling a breeze.**

Being organised does not only mean you have all your selling materials when and where you need them. It also means you have everything all taken care of – including the possible questions your customer may throw at you. You have to make sure that for the simplest and the most common of questions, you have the answers handy, either in the back of your mind or on a brochure. Fumbling around for papers and solutions won't do you any good. Your customer might get impatient and change his mind about buying.

3. **Take advantage of the power of good testimonials.**

Good customer service will tell you that you don't forget a customer right after every sale. Instead, follow them and help them with anything about the product or answer questions about its use. It is also a good time to ask for feedback as to whether they are satisfied with the sale, both regarding the commodity and the quality of support or customer service they received. You can even ask some of your all-too-pleased customers for good testimonials. More often than not, they will be very willing to vouch for a good word or two about you, the product they bought, and the company that made it.

4. **Update your sales materials regularly.**

If you are indeed using catalogues, visual aids, brochures, and leaflets, you have to make sure that they are all up-to-date and accurate. Your customers are going to use the information contained in them to guide them with their purchases. They may even use the data you gave and compare it with your competitor's products.

Now, if you give them inaccurate data, you can expect either one of two results. The first result: your customer will choose another product over yours because what you have doesn't fair well when compared to others. This will likely happen if you haven't updated your materials with the innovations and improvements the manufacturer has made with the product you are offering. And the second result: your customer will buy your product, thinking yours is better than the others, only to find out they are fooled because of the inaccurate facts and figures placed on the brochure they took home with them. In either case, you will end up losing. On both counts, you lose a sale because the second customer is very likely to request a refund.

5. **Talk to your customer and involve them in every moment of the pre-sale, but stop talking when he has made a purchase.**

Again, don't give your customer any second to reconsider buying. Before he makes up his mind about buying a particular product, continue talking to the customer. Good conversation skill is what every good salesperson possesses. Don't put it to waste. Use it all the time. Besides, customers can assess right there and then if you are genuinely willing to help them make a good purchase or if you are just there to get their money. But after they decided to buy, stop talking about that particular product. Remember, they can always change their mind, walk out of the store, and leave you dumbfounded. The smart thing to do is ask them if they would be interested in an "advanced" version of the product (if any) or if they would like a complimentary product to go with the sale (Example: Would you like fries or sundae with that meal?).

6. **Provide your customer only with the best possible product and sales deal.**

A good salesperson does not think of what he can get out of each sale he makes. He also thinks about the person on the other end of the bargain. A salesperson should strive to understand what his customer wants fully. He has to help him make an informed decision among his legitimate options. Selling is also about caring and trust. This is the primary reason why customers keep coming back.

7. **Motivate your customer to act.**

Well, don't just stand there talking to your customer about the product's benefit like a broken record. Your constant pitch will irritate your customer. Instead, drive them to buy. Make them understand that it is a lot better to own the product's benefits rather than just to hear about it. Goad them to act. Have them complete the sale.

8. **Attempt to sell related products or services to satisfied customers.**

A happy customer may be all too willing to buy other products. For example, if you are selling designer clothes to prospects and in the end, they did buy one of your products, try to sell them designer shoes and bags to match. They may not buy right away, but it is such a great opportunity to present the other products that complement the item they've purchased. You will then have an active list of customers in the future.

9. **Reach out to your most likely clients and get referrals.**

After understanding your target market, you should know precisely the type of people that will buy what you are selling. Get to meet them and sell to them aggressively. However, the meeting goes, either you got a sale or not, get referrals. They will indeed have other friends in the same field that may be willing to buy. Always make every meeting worth it, even if you did not strike a deal at all.

10. **Give your customers subsequent sales support.**

Sales support comes in various forms. It could be as simple as a telephone inquiry or as complex as a home service. Either the case or whether it is your job or not, offer assistance when it is asked of you. The least you can do is to direct them to the right support group to handle their concerns. If there is no such group, help them as much as your company policies can allow. Always keep in mind that one unhappy customer can create more damage than ten happy customers can repair.

Using Effective Sales Tools to Realise Your Goal

Today, there are a lot of tools and avenues to make yourself known and reach as many customers as you can. These tools are essential in your business because they can hoist you up the sales ladder and lead you to your first million.

1. *The Telephone*

The telephone is a vital business tool. It is widely used right now by both small-scale businesses to large corporate empires. Call centres are set up everywhere, even carried offshore to maximise cost and efficiency. Why? It's because the telephone is very powerful. You can inquire about a product through phone, place and confirm orders, and collect payment through this device. As a salesperson, you can reach your possible customers without leaving your home or office. You can talk to them at their most convenient time, without worrying about travelling, what to wear, and where to meet up. All you have to do is to press a few numbers on the keypad, wait for the person to answer on the other end of the line, and you have a deal brewing right under your nose.

2. *Local Community Groups*

To realise your goal much faster than expected, you have first to reach the local groups with which they belong. It would help if you became known in the local community you would like to penetrate first. You have to build your reputation well. And you will benefit most if you use the power of word of mouth. If everything goes well, you might not have to go to your customer at all. They would be coming to you instead.

3. *Advertising and Publicity*

Publicity will take you miles closer to your targets. Publicity includes the tri-media, as it is more known today. The newspapers and other printed materials, the television stations, and the radio airwaves are the things that correspond to publicity. Spots for these may not come free, but it is worth the investment, especially if you get to make your product or service known to the masses. If you are lucky, you might just come across some of them at no cost at all. Whichever the case, you have to make sure that you choose the one that reaches your most probable customers. Don't be too overeager and buy a television commercial spot right away only to find out that you've placed your ads for car paints on a fashion TV show, which does not jive at all.

4. *Direct Mail*

There had been a time when direct mail is a breakthrough in mass marketing. Direct mail straightforwardly informs your customers of your sales activities and promotional offers that come with it. Direct mail connects you to the very people you want to contact. It fixes on a very personal level what your customer cannot easily resist.

5. *Sales Promotional Materials*

These are your massively produced paraphernalia, usually paperwork. Your brochures, leaflets, and inserts are what compose this category. If you want to reach as many audiences as possible without caring so much for pre-qualifying, this is the way to go. Print out thousands of leaflets and scatter them all over town. Call the local newspaper dealer and strike a deal with them, putting your inserts to all periodicals for a certain fee.

Of the three, brochures are quite different. Some brochures are printed on glossy paper and usually come coloured. You don't want to put these to waste by just giving them to somebody who is not at all interested. In essence, you have to give this only to the people who are opting to buy or are most likely to buy.

6. *The Internet*

Currently, no marketing tool is as powerful as the Internet. The Internet is an avenue for everything. And it is so popular even kids know how to use it. The Internet is where everybody virtually meets. If you want to market your products to the rest of the world, you can use the Internet. And it is the most inexpensive way to do it. Today, everything can be done online. You can advertise, sell your product, and receive payment, all without leaving the comforts of your home or office. All you need is some knowledge of how e-commerce and internet marketing works, and get ready to be swept away by voluminous orders.

The Qualities of an Excellent Salesperson

Being a salesperson should be easy. That is if you have all the qualities of a good salesperson in you. However, you do your job, whether face-to-face, over the telephone, or through the Internet, you must possess all these qualities. Once you do, sales and commissions will keep on pouring in, and you will need an extra hand fulfilling orders.

1. Neatness and Presentability

For a salesperson, image is everything. It is true that before you get to sell anything, you always have to sell yourself first. And that means you should be highly likeable before you get somebody to like your products. Giving your possible customers a wrong impression of you won't help at all. It would help your competitors, though, because it takes you out of the picture.

You won't always know your customers personally. You will be meeting a lot of them, if not all of them, only once in your life. And that means you will be approaching them and talking to them as a total stranger. In this case, they might be scrutinising you in an attempt to judge what kind of a person you are. And they might do that mostly based on your looks alone.

It is, therefore, important that you look neat and presentable all the time. Your aura and your physical image tell a lot about who you are and the company you represent. People do not like to deal with somebody they do not feel comfortable with. Unruly hair and dirty teeth could make you lose a sale. Don't take the risk. Invest in your appearance. But this doesn't mean you have to buy and wear expensive suits all the time. Good grooming will make you stand out even if your clothes are old. Just make sure they are well kept, and you should be fine.

2. Professionalism

Professionalism is how you do things right. For starters, you should not be irritating. Certain habits or conducts annoy some people. If you have a nasty habit like fidgeting with your fingers, cutting somebody's sentence off, playing with your pen, or talking too fast, you have to do your best to eliminate it. As a rule of thumb, any habit that you think may annoy somebody else has to go – and do it in any way possible. If you have to undergo therapies to get rid of it, do it. Much of your career depends on it. Keep in mind that the selling career entails person-to-person contact. Because of that, you have to do everything to create a good impression and comfortable air between you and your customer.

3. Good Listening Skills

More than anything, a customer would like to be heard and understood, sometimes at all costs. To be a good salesperson, you have to develop your ability to listen, even to the words left unsaid. Let your customer talk. After all, they come to you because they want something. Hear them out and show them that you correctly understood what they are trying to convey. You may uncover a behaviour or attitude that can propel you to make a sale. If you fail to do so the first time, don't hesitate to ask them again. This will show that you are concerned about what they are saying and you don't want to miss a detail. But don't do it many times in a conversation, or else, the customer will assume that you are not paying attention.

4. **Sensitivity**

Always put yourself in your customer's shoes. This is the only way you can feel what it is that concerns them and what they are trying to make you comprehend. Doing so will also ensure that you are on the right ground when it comes to dealing with people. Some salespeople become too overeager to collect the commissions they would get out of every sale that they forget to treat their customers with utmost care and attention. This is the gravest mistake you can make as a salesperson. The moment you regard your customers as one-time deals is the moment you can say goodbye to your career. With that attitude, even your most loyal clients will break out and leave you hanging by a thin line eventually.

5. **Enthusiasm**

Enthusiasm is infectious. If you're excited about your product and the benefit it can give, your customers would soon follow suit. They would see your product differently, enough to complete a sale. Good salespeople are cheerful and passionate about their craft. You should develop these qualities right at the start of your career.

6. Knowledge

This doesn't mean that you necessarily need to have above-average comprehension skills to start with. It means being smart with a good ability to grasp data. When a good salesperson sells his product, he knows all its prime qualities by heart. He makes it a point that he has the answer to the most asked - about the question concerning the product he is selling at the back of his mind. He does not grope around looking for answers when somebody pops them up. Instead, he comes prepared with a smart solution all the time.

7. Integrity

Integrity means honesty and doing the right things, even when somebody is not looking at you. Many customers want to stay clear of a deceitful salesperson. That is the reason why they size salespeople up before they attempt to buy or even before asking anything about the product. Customers want to know exactly how the product works, without any tall lies and truth-bending. They only want to deal with a straight, honest salesperson.

8. Courtesy

Courtesy is something everybody appreciates. Customers want to be treated like kings. They may bombard you with questions before they decide to buy, or they can try all your products before selecting the one right for them. Customers have varying tastes and styles. As a salesperson, part of your job is to conform to all their eccentricities. You might need to practice patience and be good-natured. Always remember that the most likeable salesperson still gets the job done.

9. Persuasiveness

All salespeople are required to be persuasive. They should be able to effectively convince their customers about the beauty of the product they are selling within appropriate levels. They should not drop at every block the customer throws at them. Instead, they should look at it as a challenge that they have to overcome. Most highly successful salespeople are even looking forward to all these challenges. They feel triumphant with every sale if they can prevail over the customer's negativities. This is something that adds excitement and stimulation to their job.

CHAPTER FOUR

Handling Objections

A lot of people assume that selling is not easy. And that's because of the numerous objections potential customers will shoot at you whenever you attempt to contact or talk to them to start a sale. Some objections may be given as the sale presentation, or sales pitch is in progress. But little do they know that some of these objections, like the price of the product or the service that comes with it, could very well be an indication of a customer's interest in buying.

If you think about it, your customers won't object to how high your product's price is if they have not considered the possibility of owning it. Therefore, you must take on all their objections accordingly and convert them to your benefit. Over time, different new techniques are being developed to handle the customer's every single objection. The ones listed below are the most effective ways as practised by thriving salespeople.

1. The Boomerang Technique

The goal of this technique is to turn the customers around by taking exactly what they said to you, only to show that they are mistaken in their argument. It is called the boomerang technique because you use their opinions like a boomerang. They go around in a full circle, and when they come back, you are there to persuade them again.

A good example of a boomerang technique is as follows:

Customer:*I think this necklace is costly.*

Salesperson*: I do believe it is too. But I assume that you don't want to give your wife a much cheaper present. Anyway, the necklace comes in a beautiful case and a rebate coupon. It is a lovely present as it is. And even if you don't have the cash to pay for it today, we accept other payment methods like credit cards or even personal checks, though that requires some time to clear. And we can reserve this piece for you so that nobody else can buy it before you do.*

The main idea here is to first agree to what customers are saying to make them believe that they are right. Then you try to attach what you, as a salesperson, want to impart. By doing that, you are using the principle of association. What you say simply becomes correct as well.

Renaming the Objections

There may even be times that the customer's objection can be turned into positive energy outright. If the customer says that they have to talk to their husband or wife before they make a purchase or that they don't have the money to buy it right now, you don't just leave that as is and let them go with it. Instead, you handle it by making a play with words. Check out the example below:

Customer:*I think I like your product, but I can't buy it right now, as I don't have the money. I would need to **tell**my husband about it and see what he says.*

Salesperson:*Yes, I suppose that's proper, but instead of doing that, could you rather **discuss**it with him so that I can finalise your order today? I can arrange for somebody to pick up the payment tomorrow for you.*

As you can see, "tell" and "discuss" almost mean the same thing. But "discuss" is a much stronger word than "tell". To effectively close a sale, you should always use the more powerful word. You don't change their meaning, but you have successfully translated them more in your favour.

Show the Customers the Bigger Picture

There are times when there is a need to show your customers that small and insignificant things are precisely that – insignificant. Make their objection about the colour of the product look trivial compared to its portability or any of its other robust features. The technique here is to show to the customer what they can get in contrast to what they can't. But don't dwell on the things that your product can't give. Focus more on the things it can offer.

Here's an example:

Customer:*I think this laptop is too big for me. I would like to buy something more compact.*

Salesperson: *You might have a point there. But this laptop is complete. It comes with everything you would need on a computer. What are a few inches in size if it can give you full functionality?*

Try to distract your customers from the issue that you cannot resolve like size, shape, weight, and similar objections. Create an entirely different perspective on your product. Make it appear the best buy despite the small detail the customer requires.

Reframing the Objection

Reframing the objection is very similar to saying "no" to the customer in an entirely different way. You can do it by showing that there's a misunderstanding between both of your views. Use empathy. Blame the misunderstanding of yourself. Try turning the subject around as you reframe the objection. Read the following example:

Customer:*You don't seem to understand. I do not like this one. What I wanted is a long coat. This one looks a little short on me.*

Salesperson:*Oh yes, sorry about that. But I just can't help suggesting this one to you. It looks good on your body frame.*

Use the same terms or jargon the customers used on you to show that you understand what they need. But specifically, show them your viewpoint so that it will be difficult for them to deny that you are also right.

2. The Conditional Closing Technique

The idea behind this technique is simple. Don't give your customers a second to think about possible objections. Instead of saying "Would you like to step in and check our products?" You say, "If you would step inside our booth and see our products, you are sure to find exactly what you are looking for. The following is another good example.

Customer:*I want a portable-type DVD player. I think you don't have any stock available.*

Salesperson:*If I call up the head office for delivery right now, the portable DVD player should be here in less than an hour. Will you wait for it?*

See here that the conversation goes assertive, but it doesn't impose upon the customer. Try to build an agreement with your customer. Use the agreement that behind the surface says, "If I can solve the setback, you should buy the product."

An even more robust method is to structure your question in such a way that they will think they have options, yet both of these options are directed towards a sale. Ask questions like, "Would you like to pay in cash or credit card?" or "Would you like to take it home with you or have it delivered by us?" In these cases, any reply would result in a sale.

Repulsing the Objection

This is the bold type of objection. This technique involves telling the customer subtly that they are wrong. But even though this objection is rather forceful, it does not necessarily mean aggressive. Tell the customer that they are wrong, but do not rub it on them directly. See how the example below goes:

Customer:I believe that XYZ Company has the pioneering technology for photo printers. I suppose I should go for them to get the best buy.

Salesperson:That's not true, sir. Even though the XYZ Company is the one who is regarded to be a pioneer, it does not mean that they have the best technology in the market. Our engineering team had come up with this innovative photo printer with features that are first in its right today. I'm sure you won't see anything like it and all its capabilities in any of our competitor's product lines.

Did you see how assertively yet feebly the salesperson handled the objection of the customer? That's exactly how to do it. Politely tell that the customer that they are wrong and prove it to them. Prove it by making your products shine out. Besides, showing the customer that they are wrong will reveal how much you know about your product and would expose your customer to their deception (should they use one as an objection to creating a way out).

3. **The Curious Salesperson Technique**

Some customers can say point-blank to you that they do not want to buy what you are selling. Try to act curious and ask them why. They might stumble upon some reasons that they might have thought about at that minute.

Take each reason as an objection you can readily handle. Even if the customer did not buy, you have made contact and probably, a good acquaintance. You'll never know when the same customer will soon decide to purchase and would come looking for you. Moreover, they can spread the news about your product through word-of-mouth, which happens to be one of the best promotional methods.

Here's an example of the curious salesman technique:

Customer:*I don't think I need these drapes just yet.*

Salesperson:*A lot of people had bought from us this week since it's the holidays. I wonder why you are deciding otherwise. Was there any other reason? I'm quite sure that if you tell me, we can try to work something out.*

If you let out the child in you through inquisitiveness at the right time, you will surely either make a sale or gain a future customer. Whichever the case, you are bound to gain something from it.

Anticipating the Objection

Make your work easier by thinking about the most likely objection your product might get. Address it early on in the conversation so that it will not surface later on. This is important so that the customer won't mention it at a rather inconvenient time. Take the example below:

Customer:*I'm looking for a charm bracelet to give as a gift to my mother.*

Salesperson:*You've come to the right store, sir. Here are the best ones we've got. I know that these might cost a little. But they are made of high-quality authentic stones, making them the perfect gift for a particular person like your mother.*

See how the salesperson addressed the issue about the price of the product early on? Not only will the customer be informed that the product may not come cheap, but it can also be a gauge of whether or not the customer can afford it. If they back up immediately after saying the actual price of the product, you will know it is out of their budget. But if they don't budge, they may have the money to buy it. This is very applicable to all the other major objections customers may have about your product.

Sidetracking the Objection

Probably the easiest way to handle an objection is to wave it off. This is the best way to go if the objection is major and insurmountable. No matter how good a salesperson you are, if you are trapped with the wrong product, you can only do as much. Therefore, a way out of this kind of objection is to let it go, at least for a while. You have the option to address it later, or you can opt not to at all. Check the example below:

Customer:Your digital camera has the lowest resolution in the market today. I wonder why it is still not putting down its price regardless of other brands releasing newer models already.

Salesperson:That's a good observation. I'll give you an answer to that later. However, if you look at the type of camera lens we are using, you will see that the camera is highly durable and would last for years.

The only thing that you have to remember about deflecting the customer's question is not to shrug it off nonchalantly. Remember that customers want to be heard. So it would help if you acknowledged their objection. Show them that you have heard it and did understand what they said. They deserve that in the least, especially if you don't intend to answer their question later on.

Objection Bargaining

Objections will always arise. They are always a part of every sales transaction, no matter how big or small the deal is. One way to make objections work in your favour, instead of the customers, is to strike a deal with them early on. After their first two objections, try to tell them that you are willing to answer the rest of their doubts about the product by asking them to write all objections on a piece of paper. Then continue with your sales pitch. Here's an example.

Customer:I'd like to buy that car audio system you are selling, but I'm concerned about its installation, warranty, and almost everything else about it.

Salesperson: Well, I'd like to propose a deal with you, sir. If you listen to my presentation about the audio system, you can write down or make a mental note of all the possible questions and objections you may have about it as I go along. Then I will be addressing all of them to your satisfaction.

The example here has to be carried out in a mildly assertive manner and never in a pushy one. The customer is not supposed to feel trapped. They definitely won't like that. It is also essential to make them understand that you will be crossing off their objections only if they are satisfied with the way you handled it. Else, they are free to check out the competitor's product. You have to emphasise that point.

The Use of Empathy

You have to realise the powers of empathy. Empathy is the mental process of putting one's self into the shoes of another, and in this case, the shoes of the customers. It is a way of showing that you understand and feel the same way as your customer. Read the example below:

Customer:I am not comfortable with the fit of this blouse. I think it is too smug. I can't move much.

Salesperson:I know exactly how you feel. I tried one on and felt the same way. But I bought it and took it home instead. I wore it for the first time last night, and I felt so confident in it. It matched my skirt, and the blouse isn't too smug at all. It *showed off my curve perfectly. However, if you think a larger size fits you better, I'll be willing to help you.*

Empathy alone has the power to change minds and emotions. The key here is to be as truthful as you can. Do not lie. The customers can see through you. Remember that they have a critical eye that is always checking you out. Just a single lie and they will never come back.

The Use of Humor

Humour has its share of powers too. This is the perfect alternative to negative emotions. Instead of responding to your customer's endless and persistent objection with either anger or frustration, try humour. It will make the whole ordeal lighter and easier. You can also use humour to diffuse tension in the air, especially when things are heating up for some reason. Here's an example.

Customer:*I am just passing by admiring your dog outside the window. Now you want me to buy it. I don't intend to purchase anything. Please don't stand in my way. I've got to go, and I still have work to do.*

Salesperson:*Sir, the dog likes you now. He's telling it to me through his gentle barks. Don't you just hear the words he's saying? He's saying, "Take me home. I'd like you to be my master." In fact, why don't you give it a try? Take the dog home for a few days, and if you don't like it, you can always return it.*

Some people easily go off the hook even with slight persuasion. The trick is to learn not to get offended. That way, you won't be offending your customer with your replies. Inject a little humour whenever the situation calls for it, and your sale will proceed the way that it should. Use gentle humour as a defence against hotheaded customers. It is convenient during such times. It has proven to dissolve the customer's anger somewhat.

CHAPTER FIVE

Selling and Presenting Your Product

Almost all customers would agree in saying that the product's presentation has a lot to do with their reasons for buying. They like a very presentable product, both in its overall appearance and its packaging. Therefore, no matter how good your product is, if it is not appealing to the eye, it is not going to have market appeal. Appeal to your customer's aesthetic preferences. A lot of companies are investing so much just to improve their product design. Most of the time, a simple change in the packaging layout would translate to millions of sales. Good enough is not enough. Always settle for the best possible product appearance and packaging.

Here are the four basic principles of how your overall product presentation should look like:

- It should be attention-grabbing.
- It should be crafted to build customer's interest in the product.
- It should arouse the customer's desire to own the product.
- It should be enough to goad the customers to action.

When it comes to presentation, your main point of interest is what pleases the eye. While it is true that beauty is in the eye of the beholder, all you have to follow is to appeal to the general concept of beauty. Always stick to the conventional assumption of beauty, and you would never go wrong.

How to Attract Your Customer's Attention

Every product has a benefit. A benefit is anything your product can give to your customers. This is something you put upfront so that people will begin buying from you. To attract your customer' attention, you have to create a good selling point for every benefit your product has to give. All of those should be emanating out from your product and packaging, with or without the use of actual words.

An example of a product's benefit is portability. One selling point of this particular product feature is the use of rechargeable batteries, which enables your customers to bring the product or device wherever they go. And aside from directly stating that your product is portable, you can choose to manufacture your product in a compact design or to select a slim packaging so that buyers will see that your item can be enjoyed whenever, wherever. If one glance at your product would show that it is lightweight, condensed, and has a rugged construction fit for outdoor use, you have succeeded in attracting your customer's attention.

If in case you are a salesperson who only markets products that comes from your manufacturers and you do not have any influence as to its manufacturing design or packaging, you have to do some physical evaluation of your product before selling them. When possible, get your product and put it side by side with its competitors. Then answer these questions:

- How is your product different?
- What are the benefits your products have that others don't?
- When it comes to its physical design, what is it that the product manufacturers emphasise?
- What is stated in the packaging that should make the product saleable?

After answering these questions, you should have a good idea as to how you should present your product in the market. If you have to make your leaflets to give away to customers, then you can put all the primary selling points of your product, from the most salient ones down to the minor points. This way, you are effectively presenting your product in the market.

Product manufacturers usually perform comprehensive market research before they design and construct a product. Usually, the results of these researches are imparted to the marketing leaders, with the intention that they are passed on to every salesperson they have in force. They want these selling points to be promoted to the customers. It all depends upon you, the salesperson, to put the product's innate selling points out in the limelight. Remember to stress out the benefits (protects against all impurities, more compact, etc.) more than the features (made of durable plastic, removable filter, etc.)

How to Build Your Customer's Interest

To keep the excitement in the air, you have to keep your customers guessing. Your promotional materials should leave customers with an atmosphere of interest enough to make them ask for more. Give them something they haven't heard of before. And indeed, they would give your product a second look. This is all you need to fully launch that well-prepared and well-thought-out speech you have prepared.

Interest is something you want to trigger in your customer. Interest can do wonders. It could create a buzz about your product. It can entice more customers to check out what it is you are selling. Most importantly, it can make your customers buy, if only to check out if what they heard about the product is correct. If you can keep your customer's interest brewing, then you are on the right track. You just have to make sure that you follow it up with the right sales talk and the right promotional attack. Otherwise, the work you did to generate interest will just go to waste.

How to Arouse Your Customer's Desire

More often than not, desire is aroused by beauty, appeal, and attractiveness. Functionality and features usually come second. So, in essence, you work to stimulate your customer's desire, first through the physical attributes of your products. Its features and capabilities come second.

This may look too easy, but aesthetics is not a simple science. Aesthetics is rather vague and is very general. The adage still holds– beauty depends on the person who appreciates it. You have to keep in mind who your customers are and what their preferences might be before you can appeal to their senses. This is especially hard if you do not have any control over your product's aesthetic abilities, and you are just selling it. But we can get to that later. First, here are the different channels of attraction and how you can use them to present your product to arouse your customers' desire to buy.

1. **Vision**

The first step is to appeal to the eyes. Consumers want a product that looks good visually. Again, this is why companies are investing so much in remodelling and repackaging their products to look new and trendy. Never mind the features. They can improve on that later, or maybe never. Some companies just opt to create an entirely different model of the product instead of adding good features to it. Repackaging is always costly. But a lot do it anyway.

2. Hearing

If there's any music or sounds associated with your product and it is very engaging, capitalise on it. Let the music arouse desire. Music and sounds have the innate ability to do that. There might be times that you went walking in the mall and you heard your favourite song play somewhere. Do you remember how you stopped and just listened? You might have even walked right into the store just to enjoy the music. Music can relay a message of your product. Music uses the power of words and the melody of a good tune. That's why songs and jingles are always created and used in television commercials. People love to hear good harmony. And that's one reason why the music industry is always flourishing.

3. The Sense of Smell

What is your first reaction when you are walking in a busy street, and somebody with your favourite cologne walked right past you? You intend to look at the direction of the person, no matter how far away he may be. You might even search for his face in the crowd. Some people would even stop and savour the scent. Whichever your reaction is, the point is clearly stated. You simply can't resist the allure of a good smell. Whether it is the smell of somebody's cooking or the fragrance of your favourite perfume, you tend to turn your head even without meaning to. And that effect is something you would like to achieve for your products.

4. The Sense of Taste

This one is for products that have something to do with eating or ingesting. It could be food products, drinks, or even medicines. If it has to go through the mouth, you have to make sure it tastes good. And yes, that holds even for medications. This is something fundamental. You won't sell a chocolate bar that doesn't taste sweet, right? Therefore, if you have to sell food, you have to make sure eating it will become your taste bud's enjoyment. People like to try something new now and then. Most of them are tired of the usual taste of the food they eat. This is the reason why companies are coming out with the orange, cherry, or apple flavours of their products. You don't want to eat plain Jell-O's every morning for the rest of your life, right? Or wheat grain cereals. Or plain fruit jellies. People like some variants. So benefit from that.

5. The Sense of Touch

The sense of touch is almost as important as the sense of sight. Your product, more often than not, can indeed be touched, be felt, and be experienced by your customers. Touch applies to almost everything: shoes, clothes, equipment, furniture, appliances, and vehicles – the list goes on. And how it should feel will depend entirely on what product you are selling. If you have furniture, a smooth and sleek design is an advantage.

But if you are selling sports equipment, the handles have to be ribbed for better handling. It also has to be light and durable, especially if it's something like a tennis racket. It's a different story, though, if what you are selling is a golf club. The idea here is simple. Make sure that your product brings comfort, even if it is used for an entirely different purpose.

These are the ways on how you can appeal to your customer's senses. But what if you are still considered as a low-level salesperson, and you do not have any control of the product's aesthetic abilities? Well then, since you can't be changing your products, change the way you present your products. Answer these questions:

1. What are the selling points of your product?

2. Of them, all, which do you think is the most significant?

3. How can you promote this particular selling point?

4. Using which senses are you going to endorse the product best?

5. Can you combine two or more senses to achieve optimum results?

6. Are you creative enough to appeal to all of a person's senses?

Your choice of approach, endorsement, or advertisement is going to count a lot. Use the right one. Better yet, be imaginative enough to create your own. Make your market plan. Make your commercials, posters, and other attention-grabbing materials whenever you can. It may mean extra work, but it would surely take you closer to your goal.

How to Goad Your Customers into Action

Now, this is the meat of the matter. When we are talking about action, we mean buying. And buying is the primary goal of every sales deal. It is what every salesperson aims to get. The million-dollar question comes to the surface: How then can you make a customer buy?

After going through the steps listed in this book, you should have learned about product presentation, quality, appeal, customer's objections, and the salesman qualities. All these are taught with only one intention – that you successfully get into your customers' heads and goad them into action.

Selling is a very psychological thing. A good product won't necessarily sell without an equally good salesperson behind it. Try it. Let's do some role-playing. Get your products on the frontline and act not as an enthusiastic salesperson but as an indifferent vendor. Act like somebody who gets paid by the hour without commissions. That means you will get your salary after working hours, no matter how few or how many items you have sold. See if you are going to achieve your day's goal.

Now act like a very aggressive salesperson and take what you think is your worst product. Maybe for research, you can even select a brand or a commodity that you think is big junk. Sell it passionately, following everything taught in this report. See if you had sold more products acting like this compared to when you are acting like the uninterested salesperson.

This is the first point you have to know. Selling is not entirely about your product. Your product won't sell on its own. That is the very reason why your boss hired you in the first place. He knows it. You should know it too. Be reminded of this one thing: *Before you can sell anything, you have to sell yourself first*. This is why you are taught the qualities of a good salesperson earlier. The moment you speak to your customer about your product is the moment your customer may be doing his best trying to trust you. If he finds that very hard to do, you are in big trouble.

The second point is that not all customers buy impulsively. You might be lucky to meet more than one compulsive customer in a day. So don't gripe if the customer lets you talk for five whole hours only to leave the store without making a single purchase. This happens, and it does quite often. So you have to know your plan of attack each time you face your customer. If he is a new customer, don't come on too strong. Again, customers do not like to be pushed around and feel ensnared.

The third point: Keep your customer interested. Getting your customer's attention is not enough. You have to keep the water flowing. You have to capture their interest and sustain it. But do it in such a way that it doesn't look as though you are going to some extreme heights just to sell to them. Customers know when you are making a conversation and when you are making a sales pitch for them to buy. It is your job to keep them interested. And when their interest is at its peak, move in to close the deal. That should be the time when they are more than willing to take out their wallets right then and make the purchase.

The last and main point: Let your customer know your intentions. Make it clear to them that you wanted them to buy your product, get an insurance plan, sign up for a loan, purchase a warranty card or anything else you might want them to do. Calling them to action is not enough. They have to know what the real action is, what they are supposed to do. And be prepared for that. Don't be too engrossed in your sales pitch that you forget little details (like the customer has to have several identification cards to go with the purchase or other trivial things like that). Assess your customer while you are talking to them. Determine what they need to do and make them want to do it. Now that's the best salesperson in action!

To guide you further in your selling, here are four almost magical selling techniques that you can use to your advantage:

The Reciprocity Technique

Capitalise on people's tendency to reciprocate good thoughts and efforts. Whenever you give or do something nice to others, people are always obligated to return the favour. As a seller, give your customers holiday and greeting cards on special occasions. They will appreciate it and will buy again from you in the future. The same principle applies when you give samples or trial offers. They might buy your product just for the sake of reciprocity!

The Contrast Technique

Many people in today's world shop with a budget in mind. With the current economy, it doesn't pay to be a spendthrift. To overcome this obstacle (in case your product has a higher price), show your prospective customer the super value they can get from your product in contrast to your competitors' (which could be priced lower). Let them realise and feel the excellent quality they are getting in exchange for a few dollars more.

The Herd Technique

Most people like to belong to a group. They want to do what the rest of humankind is doing, so they can feel a sense of belonging. In restaurants, they may apply this principle by giving free foods and massive discounts to their customers. If people see that there are many people inside a diner, they won't hesitate to go inside themselves. The same is true with discos and bars. Long lines are an indication that people enjoy going and hanging out at that place.

The Consistency Technique

Try to find out what your customers' preferences are. Ask them if they value quality over price. If they say "yes," that's your cue to ask them if they are willing to buy your product if it has a lot more useful features than others. People like to be consistent with their values and beliefs. And to stay consistent, they are most likely going to buy your product to prove that they indeed value quality over price.

Use these selling techniques, and you will surely get your customer buying with lesser efforts and skill required!

CHAPTER SIX

Closing the Deal

A sales deal is composed of three parts. The first part is the introduction of products to prospective customers. The second is the buying customer's acceptance of the product. And the third part, and the most important part at that, is the closing. With that said, closing is the hardest part of every sales transaction.

The work is done, and the pipelines are laid in the first two parts of the deal are where. But if your closing is weak, all those time spent in building the sale will be lost. And so, to become a good salesperson, you have to develop a strong deal closing technique. This part of the deal is very critical that some companies hire two sets of salespeople – the front liners and the closers.

But if you are a real deal salesperson like what this report is training you to become, you are the embodiment of these two. It means that you can initiate, develop, and close a deal in one fluid action. Before we go to the different techniques, you can use to close a sale, and you have to know first the five basic principles of a sale.

Timing is important.

Once you feel that the sales agreement between you and your customer is reached, you have to act swiftly. Let them sign the necessary forms and supply the required information needed to process the sale. Don't give them even a split second to change their minds. Treat the moment that they say "yes" as a bell chiming, which signifies that you are just a few moments away from victory.

Learn the proper timing in closing the deal.

If time is important, then timing is of paramount concern too. As a good salesperson, you should act at the right instant. If you act too soon or too late, you might lose a sale before you even had the chance to bat one of your eyelashes. And to keep yourself from guessing when the right time to pounce on the deal will be, always try turning the tables around in your favour. Instead of your customers dictating the pace of the transaction, you take over. But before you can do that, your sensitivity should be at work all the time.

If you feel that your customers are only half-decided, encourage them towards the right path. You can entice them by giving more discounts, offering freebies, extending warranties, and things like that. You have to lead your customer to the end of the deal. If they seem to be backing out, try one or two different moves, not desperation moves but persuasive moves. You still have to maintain the dignity of your products. Remember that you don't have to go too low for sale. You are offering your customers a good product. If they won't buy it, it is their loss. But because you are concerned for them, you are still offering them a last chance to purchase the product. An option that may not be provided to them some other time.

Bluffing sometimes works.

While this may be true, don't overdo it. If you are selling a prime property, for example, you are not supposed to tell your customer that you might call somebody who is more willing to accept what you just offered him. The instant they thought they were regarded unimportantly is the moment they walk out. Using the threat of their possible competition would show who among your customers want the product that you are selling more. Use bluffing as a tool to gauge your customer. Anyway, the customer will, more often than not, respond honestly to your bluffs. Just make sure that you ditch bluffing if it failed to work the first time.

Know what to say after they decided to buy.

As mentioned in a previous chapter, the smart thing to do is ask them if they would be interested in an "advanced" or "deluxe" version of the product (if any) or if they would like a product that compliments the main product. (Example: Would you like this cool pair of socks that match perfectly with your shoes?)

Not all sales deals lead to a close.

The sales figures for almost all companies would show that the ratio between the number of potential customers and the number of closed deals are miles apart. But this doesn't mean that you have to succumb to the numbers. As a good salesperson, you have the power to raise the percentages to considerable heights.

The Different Deal Closing Techniques

Closing the deal means taking the customer into the stage of commitment. This is where they buy – where they put out their hard-earned, and the not-so-hard earned cash for that matter, to buy your products. Therefore, to ensure you of a tightly sealed deal, here are some closing techniques you can take advantage of:

Using the Power of Assumption Technique

Act like your customer has decided to buy already. Speak confidently that what you are saying is what you believe you have understood from the conversation with the customer. Ask him directly as to how many items he would like to purchase and when he would like them delivered. If you say it appropriately, your customer will answer your question in complete detail. And when he does, be prepared to document the sale and complete it.

Sample Spiels:

So, where would you like to place these shelves once it gets in your apartment? Which of these two sizes of the bed should I process for delivery?

Using a Testimonial to Close the Deal

A happy customer is always your best advertisement. If your customer needs a little more pushing, you can state the name of one of your rather popular and highly satisfied clients, with their permission, of course. Don't forget to mention the details of the sale, like what he purchased and why he was happy. Sometimes, a customer need not know who exactly became satisfied with the product. Most of the time, hearing a good story about it from any user is enough to get them to buy. And this is especially true if they trust you as a salesperson.

Sample Spiels:

You know Mr Johns, the Vice President for Purchasing of ABC Company, regularly buys from us. You can ask him how he finds our products.

We have many regular customers up north. If you like, you can ask about our products from one of your friends there. They surely have heard about us.

The First-Hand Experience Technique

To finally get your customers buying, show them your product. Let them experience owning it, even for a few minutes. Just make sure that you do it in such a way that they would feel attached to the product even after that short moment. Show them the features that would astound them. Give them the evidence that what you are selling all along is real and accurate. With the product in their hands, they will have the opportunity to test it and eliminate any doubts that they may have about it.

Sample Spiels:

Try one of our kinds of stuff and see for yourself. Let me demonstrate what this thing can do for you. I was amazed the moment I knew about this product. Hold it. Feel how light it is. Take this home with you and return it if you feel it's not right for you.

Showing them The Better End of The Deal Closing Technique

This is the traditional deal closer. What a salesperson does here is that he shows the customer what other stuff and bonuses he will be getting the moment he buys the product. Along with that are all the other values they are going to enjoy along with the purchase. This closing is going to be effective only if all the right good-sounding words are used. You can go down further, enumerating all the details. Your goal here is to impress the customer. And impressed they should be, not bored with your droning on, about features and user's instructions. All you have to do is to repeat all the essential things that you might have already said. This will give your customer the impression that you are summarising what both you have talked about, and the only thing left to do is for him to take out his wallet.

Sample Spiels:

So that means you will get to enjoy the product and all its features, plus we will deliver it to you for free. And you are entitled to an all-inclusive lifetime technical support at no additional cost to you.

The whole package comes with an easy-to-carry duffel bag where you can store the product or take it with you anywhere. An extra set of batteries and a cleaning device are also included.

Using the Emotions Technique

If there is anything powerful in a person, that will be his emotions. To get your customer to a successful close, aim at his feelings. Specifically stir up some deep-seated sentiments that would move him the most. Observe if he is going to react positively or negatively to it. Act according to your observation. It is always safe to go for positive emotions, but in odd circumstances, going for the negative ones can benefit as well. Whenever in doubt, don't proceed.

Keep in mind that your customer's buying decision depends upon what he feels. He will buy if he feels the need or even the want for your product. He won't buy at all if he is harbouring no important feelings about what you are selling. So early on the deal, try to check out now and then what your customer feels, and see how you can use it in your closing later on.

Sample Spiels:

My previous customers told me their self-confidence increased because of the significant effects produced by this machine. Other customers are calling me, saying that they should have bought this sooner.

Using the Short-Term Offer Technique

As a last effort to close the deal with your customer, offer them some get-it-now-or-never deals. Give them discounts that hold only if they purchase before a specific period. Give them freebies to go with their product when they pay for it now. These are good baits for a customer who is having difficulty deciding whether he should buy or not. If they feel the urgency, and that they need to decide now if they want to get the offer, they would find time to do so. You will be amazed that some would even purchase your product even before you finish your sentence because they're afraid of missing something.

Moreover, if you make them believe that the product is scarce or limited, you increase the value of the product you're selling. You must try your best to give him a deal that anybody would be a fool to let go of.

Sample Spiels:

Take the product today, and I will slash an additional 5% discount. I should get approval for that, but since my boss is out for a short break, I think I can let that offer through. What do you say?

This is the last day of the sale. Tomorrow, the products are going back to their original prices. I say you take advantage of it now while the offer's still here.

Only one more model, 9850, is available. This must be your lucky day. If you miss it, it can take months before we can get new models.

Focus on the Quality Technique

This particular technique is going to work if your product's main selling point is its quality and not anything else. This means that the product may be priced considerably the highest in the market, and you can't possibly compete nor argue when it comes to that area. Therefore, the way to close the deal is to always emphasise the product's superiority, in contrast to all other factors. Affirm to him that quality matters most, that its price and all the other factors associated with it are not essential factors after all. Show customers how quality will work for them and how well the company keeps its promises when it comes to the product's performance. What you are focusing on is the product's long-term value. That is precisely what the customer is paying for.

Sample Spiels:

You only have to pay for the product once, but you get a lifetime guarantee. This is the product with the best quality out in the market today. You won't regret it. And you will soon realise that its cost is such a small price to pay.

Steps to an Effective Closing

Now that you know the basics, as well as the right methods on how to deliver the particular closing you chose, here now are the step-by-step ways to end a sale properly.

Deliver your closing.

Choose the right closing technique and deliver it well. Always aim for a close, even though the deal is improbable to end as a sale. Anyway, you can always use the practice or amusement even.

Pause for a few seconds.

After delivering your spiel, give your customers a few seconds to throw in any last-minute questions at you or to say "yes" to the deal. Don't keep on talking that you missed the consent that you have meant to hear all along.

Observe your customer's emotions.

As you talk, observe at what part of your sales talks, your customer usually responds or interrupts. And when they speak, listen to them and watch the emotions that come with their words. Use the same sentiments to lead you to a sale.

Finish the sale.

If you have said the right words to go with the correct responses, your customer will be signing the sales slip easily. But sometimes, the deal cannot be closed in a day. A big-budget deal would take weeks, months, or even years to complete. Whichever the case, just be prepared with your closing. Be armed with the right tools and the right equipment. You don't want to lose a sale because of mere irresponsibility on your part.

Thank the customer.

You have to thank the customer for the purchase. And along with that, wish him the best with his new product, offer support, and give additional pointers to do when he gets to use it. You might be the one to congratulate here on your excellent work of completing the sale, but the least you can do is to share your success with your customer by merely thanking him.

Conclusion

We have come to the end of this report. By now, you should have learned all that it takes to become a top-notch salesperson. If you follow all the things that are written here religiously, your first million will be waiting for you very soon enough.

A good salesperson who knows what he wants will reap the rewards of becoming financially stable and satisfied with his career. Selling is a career. And you can be outstanding at it. Learn the skills, follow the steps, and enjoy successfully closed sales deals day after day after day.

Always learn the true essence of selling by heart. Selling is not all about deceiving customers; it is not about manipulating your customers either. Selling is interaction. It involves talking to customers, becoming friends with them, winning their trust, and selling them your product.

You do not have to be loud-mouthed and over-ambitious to succeed as a salesperson. Instead, you have to be a person of subtle character and grace. Maintain your poise as well as those of your products. Once you and your products attained that particular level of respect, you are very likely to make sales, sometimes even without trying so hard.

Think of a good salesperson that you know of. It could be your boss or somebody in the marketing field you admire the most. It could even be somebody from the local store from whom you find yourself buying most often. Observe them. What do you think are the things that they are doing right, which makes you admire them? Do you think they are honest? Are they good at explaining? How do they talk about their product? How effective are their sales pitches on you?

You will learn a lot from a mentor. What this book teaches you are the basics, the theories, and the secrets of becoming a top-notch salesperson. Observing a good salesperson in action will show you more clearly how successful selling is done.

Right now, you should have realised that being a salesperson might not happen overnight; or it might, depending on your determination and skill. It takes practice and patience. If you follow everything this report teaches, you can become a top-notch salesperson in the shortest time possible.

If you combine all these with regular practice and determination, you will not just become a top-notch salesperson very soon. Still, you might even be heading your group of salespeople to train and manage. So keep in mind that the opportunities won't end for you if you love your craft.

Learn from this good story about an excellent salesperson:

A young guy from Texas moves to California and is looking for a job in a big department store. The manager asks whether he has some sales experience. He said that he was a salesman in Texas before he moved. The manager asked him to report the next day. He will be hired depending upon his sales for the day.

The following day, the young guy managed to get only one sale. The manager was dissatisfied with his turnout. So he said, "Our salespeople here averages 25 sales in a day. If you can only sell one item, I can't take you in."

But the guy said, "It was a $100,000 purchase, though." The manager was surprised and asked, "Really? What did you sell him?"

"Well, I sold him some biking apparel. Then I gave him a helmet. But I learned that he doesn't have a mountain bike yet, so I showed him one of ours. He bought one. He chose the biggest and heaviest model, and he found out that it won't fit in his car's trunk. He also said he doesn't know how to ride it yet, so he can't bring it home with him. So I showed him one of our trucks and sold that to him too. I told him he could take the bicycle home with it."

"You mean to tell me you successfully sold a bike to somebody who doesn't know how to ride one? And you even managed to make him buy a truck just to take it home? Why is he looking for biking apparel anyway if he doesn't know how to ride a bike?" asked the manager, bewildered.

"Well actually, he was just buying a pair of roller skates for his kid. But I told him I might as well join him in his hobby. And since he said he's too old to skate, I suggested he might as well ride a bike. He took it, so I sold all of those items to him."

See how a good salesperson can work wonders? Now, get your gear going and start earning your first million. Stop reading and start working your way up to the sales corporate ladder where you really ought to be. Conquer the selling challenge today.

www.ingramcontent.com/pod-product-compliance
Lightning Source LLC
Chambersburg PA
CBHW021507210526
45463CB00002B/930